CW00728635

Events of

News for every day of the year

**The British soul group The Real Thing
arrive in Amsterdam for a concert on
13 December.**

By Hugh Morrison

MONTPELIER PUBLISHING

Front cover The final Lunar mission, Apollo 17. David Cassidy. The first computer arcade game, Pong. The Ford Granada. David Bowie as Ziggy Stardust.

Back cover Paul Nicholas in *Jesus Christ Superstar*. The Copernicus satellite. The Airbus A30. The first scientific calculator. The Polaroid camera. The cast of *M*A*S*H*. The wreck of the RMS *Queen Elizabeth*.

Image credits: Eduard Marmet, Tom Richardson, Nyaah, UPI Photos, Alan Watkin, Gage Skidmore, Bert Verhoeff/Anefo, David Shankbone, Gil Zetbase, Ian Warren, Rick Walton, Joop van Bilson/Anefo, DOD News Features, Ford Press Office, Granada, Alf van Beem, Allan Warren, National Archives of Australia, Marion S Trikosko, Mr RF, Albin Olsson, Benjamin Goetzinger, Getty Images, The Supermat, UPI, Exshow, Giorgio Lotti, Lisbon Museum of Art, Cogart Strangehill, That Hartford Guy, Skybird 73, Rob Mieremet, Thomas Bakka, Chris Rand, Tasnim, Monster 471, Geoff Charles/National Library of Wales, Barry Loigmann, Hans Peters/Anefo, George Chernilevsky.

Published in Great Britain by Montpelier Publishing.
Printed and distributed by Amazon KDP.

ISBN: 9798459929607

January
1972

Saturday 1: Kurt Waldheim succeeds U Thant as Secretary General of the United Nations.

The French singer Maurice Chevalier dies aged 83.

Sunday 2: Jewellery worth US$4m is stolen from safety deposit boxes at the Pierre Hotel, New York City.

The American serial killer John Wayne Gacy commits the first of 33 murders.

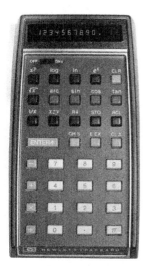

Monday 3: NASA's Mariner 9 probe begins mapping the surface of Mars.

Tuesday 4: The first scientific pocket calculator, made by Hewlett Packard, goes on sale.

Rose Heilbron becomes the first female crown court judge in England.

Wednesday 5: US President Richard Nixon announces the Space Shuttle programme.

Left: the world's first pocket scientific calculator, the HP35, is launched on 4 January.

January 1972

The wreck of the RMS *Queen Elizabeth* following a fire on 9 January.

Thursday 6: Journalist Geraldo Rivera shocks the USA with his report on conditions at New York's Willowbrook State School for children with mental disability.

Friday 7: 104 people are killed when Iberia Airlines flight 602 crashes while attempting to land on the island of Ibiza.

Saturday 8: Dmitri Shostakovich's *Symphony Number 15 in A Major* is first performed, at the Moscow Conservatory.

Sunday 9: The first nationwide coal miners' strike since 1926 begins in the UK.

The RMS *Queen Elizabeth* is destroyed by fire in Victoria Harbour, Hong Kong.

Monday 10: Bangladesh's leader, Sheikh Mujibur Rahman, is released from prison in Pakistan and returns home to a hero's welcome.

Tuesday 11: *The Night Stalker* starring Darren McGavin becomes the highest rated TV movie to this date.

Sheikh Mujibur Rahman is released from prison on 10 January.

Wednesday 12: The first regulations limiting exposure to asbestos are introduced in the USA.

Above: Red Foxx and Demond Wilson star in *Sanford and Son,* first broadcast on 14 January. **Below:** Princess Margareth of Denmark, who becomes Queen on 15 January.

Thursday 13: Lt Col Ignatius Kutu Acheampong seizes control of Ghana in a bloodless coup.

Friday 14: *Sanford and Son*, the US version of the BBC comedy *Steptoe and Son*, is first broadcast.

King Frederick IX of Denmark dies aged 71.

Saturday 15: As the Danish constitution does not permit a coronation or the wearing of a crown, Queen Margareth II of Denmark becomes Queen by simple proclamation.

Sunday 16: A solar eclipse takes place across South America and Antarctica.

Monday 17: 'Huge Monday', the 'greatest day in surfing history' takes place as 20 foot high waves hit Hawaii.

Tuesday 18: Dr Baruch S Blumberg receives a patent for a vaccine against Hepatitis B.

Wednesday 19: The Council of Europe adopts *Beethoven's Ode to Joy* as the anthem of the European Union.

The micronation of Minerva is founded off the coast of Tonga.

Thursday 20: OPEC raises the price of oil by 8.49%, the first of many steep rises leading to the first 1970s oil crisis.

Jackie Stewart, who wins the Argentine Grand Prix on 23 January.

The number of unemployed in the UK reaches one million for the first time since the 1930s.

Friday 21: Three new Indian states are created: Tripura, Manipur and Meghalaya.

Saturday 22: The UK, Ireland, Denmark and Norway sign a treaty of accession to the Common Market (later the European Union).

Sunday 23: The British Formula One champion Jackie Stewart wins the 1972 Argentine Grand Prix.

Monday 24: Sergeant Shoichi Yokoi of the Imperial Japanese army surrenders to two local fisherman on the Pacific island of Guam, having been in hiding since 1944.

Tuesday 25: Shirley Chisholm becomes the first black woman to be elected to the US Congress.

Vesna Vulović.

Wednesday 26: A Yugoslavian air stewardess, Vesna Vulović, survives a fall of 33,000 feet (more than the height of Mount Everest) after her plane is blown up by a terrorist bomb over Czechoslovakia. Miss Vulović is the only survivor of the attack and remains the world record holder for the highest fall without a parachute. She makes an almost complete recovery and dies at the age of 66 in 2016.

Thursday 27: Odyssey, the first commercial home video game system, is launched.

The first commercial home video game system, Odyssey, is launched on 27 January. The package includes the tennis game Pong shown here.

Friday 28: The opera *Treemonisha* by the ragtime pianist Scott Joplin (1868-1917) is performed for the first time after being found in 1970.

The opera *Treemonisha* by Scott Joplin *(above)* is first performed on 28 January.

Saturday 29: Known political radicals are barred from holding government office in West Germany.

Sunday 30: 14 people are killed in 'Bloody Sunday' as British troops clash with protesters in Londonderry, Northern Ireland.

Monday 31: US airlines announce that all passengers and baggage will be searched for weapons before flying.

King Mahendra Bir Bikram Shah of Nepal dies aged 51.

February 1972

Tuesday 1: The French government requests the extradition of the Nazi fugitive Klaus Barbie after it is reported he is living in Bolivia.

Wednesday 2: The British Embassy in Dublin is burnt to the ground by an angry mob in protest at the Bloody Sunday killings in Londonderry.

The US Olympic gold skier Barbara Cochran at the Winter Olympics, which opens on 3 February.

Thursday 3: The 1972 Winter Olympics opens in Sapporo, Japan.

Friday 4: Kenneth Kaunda, President of Zambia, turns his country into a one-party state after having opposition politicians arrested.

The Nazi fugitive Klaus Barbie (shown here in the 1940s) is located on 1 February.

Above: **David Bowie in the stage persona of 'Ziggy Stardust', who first appears on 10 February.**

Saturday 5: Jean-Bedel Bokassa of the Central African Republic declares himself 'President for Life.'

Sunday 6: US President Nixon attempts unsuccessfully to start secret peace talks with North Vietnamese leaders.

Monday 7: Keith Holyoake resigns as Prime Minister of New Zealand after eleven years in power.

Tuesday 8: Britain's Guardian newspaper reports on the new fashion trend of 'cheesecloth smocks' for women.

Wednesday 9: A State of Emergency is declared in the UK as supplies of coal dwindle during the nationwide miners' strike.

A seven day long blizzard ends in Iran, with up to 4000 deaths and snowdrifts of 26' high reported.

Thursday 10: David Bowie makes his first appearance as 'Ziggy Stardust', in a concert at the Toby Jug pub in Tolworth, Surrey.

Friday 11: France and Germany announce plans for financial and economic union by the 1980s.

Above: **Cheesecloth smocks hit the headlines on 8 February.**

Saturday 12: US forces conclude one of the most intensive bombing campaigns of the Vietnam War, with 356 strikes in three days.

February 1972

The VW Beetle becomes the world's best-selling car on 17 February.

Sunday 13: The 1972 Winter Olympics closes in Sapporo, Japan, with the USSR winning the most medals (eight golds).

Monday 14: US President Richard Nixon lifts the embargo on exports to China, in place for over 20 years.

Tuesday 15: ABC TV in the USA makes the first experimental broadcast with subtitles for the deaf.

The 'Cod Wars' begin as Iceland cancels its fishing treaty with the UK, banning British ships from fishing within 50 miles of its coastline.

Wednesday 16: The first package tours arrive in the Maldives since the island's independence from Britain in 1965.

Thursday 17: Britain's House of Commons votes by a narrow margin of eight to join the Common Market (later the European Union).

The Volkswagen Beetle breaks the record, previously held by the Ford Model T, as the most popular car ever built, as the 15,007,034th model is produced.

Friday 18: The death penalty is abolished in California. 107 prisoners on Death Row have their sentences reduced to life imprisonment.

Saturday 19: Union leaders recommend that members accept government proposals to end the miners' strike in the UK.

Sunday 20: US President Richard arrives in China for historic

US President Nixon meets Chinese leader Mao Tse Tung during this tour of China which begins on 20 February.

diplomatic and trade talks. He is the first US leader to visit the Peoples' Republic, ending 25 years of non-communication.

Monday 21: US President Richard Nixon meets China's Prime Minister Zhou Enlai in Beijing. Nixon later says of the meeting, 'one era ended and another began.'

Tuesday 22: Seven people, all civilians, are killed when an IRA bomb explodes at a barracks in Aldershot, in reprisal for British actions on 'Bloody Sunday', 30 January.

Emperor Haile Selassie ends the Sudanese Civil War on 27 February.

Wednesday 23: Passengers on Lufthansa Flight 649 are freed in Aden after the plane was hijacked on 22 February. The release was secured by a $5m ransom paid by the West German government.

Thursday 24: 28 men are killed in a fire on the Soviet submarine K19 in the Arctic Ocean.

Friday 25: Britain's National Union of Mineworkers votes to end their crippling strike, after accepting a 20% pay rise.

HM Queen Elizabeth II with the Sultan of Brunei on 29 February.

Saturday 26: 125 people are killed in a landslide at Buffalo Creek, West Virginia.

Sunday 27: Emperor Haile Selassie of Ethiopia signs the Addis Abbaba Agreement, bringing to an end the First Sudanese Civil War.

Monday 28: US President Richard Nixon announces a withdrawal of US forces from the Republic of China (Taiwan).

Tuesday 29: HM Queen Elizabeth II visits Brunei for the first time.

March 1972

Wednesday 1: Juan Maria Bordaberry becomes President of Uruguay.

Thursday 2: The deep-space probe Pioneer 10 is launched from Cape Canaveral. On 13 June 1983 it becomes the first man-made object to leave the solar system. Its last signal to earth is received in 2003.

Friday 3: 17 people are killed when Mohawk Airlines flight 405 crashes into a house in Albany, New York.

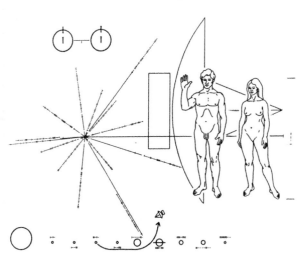

Pioneer 10, launched on 2 March, contains a pictogram plaque showing humans, chemical structures and the sun and planets of the Solar System.

The first McDonald's restaurant is demolished on 10 March. A museum reconstruction *(left)* is later built on the site.

Saturday 4: Stoke City beats Chelsea 2-1 to win the 1972 Football League Cup Final.

California lowers the age of majority from 21 to 18.

Sunday 5: Britain's Prime Minister Edward Heath announces that controversial interrogation methods for IRA suspects including deprivation of food, drink and sleep, have been banned.

Monday 6: Proceedings to deport ex-Beatle John Lennon from the USA begin.

John Lennon is given notice to leave the USA on 6 March.

Tuesday 7: A police dog named Brandy detects a bomb on TWA Flight 7 at John F Kennedy airport, New York City; the bomb is defused with 12 minutes to spare.

Wednesday 8: A further terror attack occurs on a TWA flight, when a bomb explodes on an unoccupied airliner at Las Vegas airport.

Thursday 9: US President Richard Nixon announces a new campaign of open government with fewer secrets.

Friday 10: The original McDonald's fast food restaurant, opened in San Bernadino, California, in 1940, is demolished.

Saturday 11: Protestants and Catholics clash in Portadown, Northern Ireland, after Loyalists attend an Ulster Vanguard rally.

Sunday 12: A civilian bystander is killed when IRA gunmen open fire on a British Army patrol in Belfast, Northern Ireland.

Monday 13: The US novelist Clifford Irving is charged with conspiracy to defraud, after admitting that he made up his biography of the billionaire Howard Hughes.

Tuesday 14: 112 people are killed when Sterling Airways flight 267 crashes in Dubai.

Wednesday 15: The Francis Ford Coppola film *The Godfather* is released in the USA.

Thursday 16: President Nixon proposes a moratorium on the controversial practice of 'busing' (compulsory racial de-segregation) in US schools.

Nine people are killed in a 160-car pile-up in fog on the M1 motorway in Luton, Bedfordshire.

Friday 17: In a speech to the Christian Socialist Movement in London, MP Tony Benn calls for a referendum on British membership of the Common Market.

The long-running TV series *Bewitched* ends on 25 March.

March 1972

Vicky Leandros wins Eurovision on 25 March.

Saturday 18: Larry Miller of the Carolina Cougars achieves the highest ever score (67 points) in an American Basketball Association game.

Sunday 19: The Indo-Bangladeshi peace treaty is signed in Dhaka, Bangladesh.

Monday 20: 24 climbers are killed in an avalanche on Mount Fuji, Japan.

Tuesday 21: Georgios Papadopoulos appoints himself Regent of Greece following the abdication of King Constantine II in 1967.

Wednesday 22: The US Supreme Court rules that unmarried persons have the same rights to contraception as those who are married.

Thursday 23: The Tasaday Hoax takes place, when an 'undiscovered' tribe of cave people is said to have been found in the Philippines. The fraud is not revealed until 1986.

Friday 24: The British government suspends home rule in Northern Ireland, closing the Stormont parliament in Belfast and abolishing the post of Prime Minister of Northern Ireland.

Left; the lithographer MC Escher, famouse for his 'impossible' drawings, dies on 27 March.

Top: Georgios Papadopoulos becomes Regent of Greece on 21 March. Above: the Rt Hon Priti Patel is born on 29 March.

Saturday 25: The US TV comedy series *Bewitched* ends after 254 episodes.

Luxembourg's Vicky Leandros wins the Eurovision Song Contest with Après Toi.

Sunday 26: Britain agrees to a tripling in rent for use of its military bases in the former colony of Malta, after left-wing prime minister Dom Mintoff threatens to give them to the Soviets instead.

Monday 27: The Soviet Venusian probe Venera 8 is launched.

The Dutch lithographer MC Escher dies aged 73.

Tuesday 28: The first elections in the Palestinian territory of the West Bank since 1963 are held, under Israeli supervision.

Wednesday 29: West Berliners are permitted to cross into East Berlin for a five day period, the first opening of the Berlin Wall since 1966.

The film producer J Arthur Rank dies aged 83.

The British Home Secretary Priti Patel is born in London.

Thursday 30: North Vietnam launches the Easter Offensive, a large scale invasion of South Vietnam.

Friday 31: A media sensation begins when a mysterious carcass of a large animal is found floating in Loch Ness, Scotland. Experts later find the body is not that of 'Nessie,' but of an elephant seal, placed there as a hoax by an employee of a zoo in Scarborough.

April
1972

Saturday 1: The first national baseball strike takes place in the USA, with all National and American league games cancelled in a dispute over pensions which lasts two weeks.

Sunday 2: The Republic of Ireland's second radio station, RnaG, goes on the air.

Monday 3: The actor Charlie Chaplin makes his first visit to the USA in over twenty years, to receive his Academy Award for services to the film industry.

Tuesday 4: *John Craven's Newsround*, one of the first and longest running news programmes for children, is launched on BBC1.

Left: the Ford Granada is launched on 6 April.

Wednesday 5: Six people are killed when a tornado hits Portland, Oregon.

Thursday 6: Ford launches the Granada saloon car in Britain, as a replacement for the Zephyr model.

Friday 7: United Airlines flight 855 is hijacked en route from Newark to Los Angeles. The plane lands in San Francisco and the passengers are released in exchange for $500,000; the hijacker Richard McCoy Jr escapes by parachute over Utah, but is apprehended two days later.

Saturday 8: Kjell Isaacson sets the world pole vault record at 18'1" (5.5m).

Sunday 9: The Iraqi-Soviet Treaty of Friendship is signed in Baghdad.

Monday 10: Over 5,000 people are killed in an earthquake in the province of Fars, Iran.

Tuesday 11: The long-running BBC radio panel show *I'm Sorry I Haven't a Clue* begins on Radio Four.

Wednesday 12: The Chinese table tennis team begins a tour of the USA.

Thursday 13: Following a huge search operation, Lt Col Iceal Hambleton, USAF, is rescued after being shot down and spending 11 days behind enemy lines in Vietnam.

Lt Col Hambleton is rescued on 13 April after 11 days behind enemy lines.

Friday 14: Twenty bombs are exploded and nine people killed in IRA attacks in Belfast.

April 1972

Saturday 15: A state of civil war is declared in Uraguay.

Sunday 16: The first giant pandas in the USA, Ling-Ling and Hsing-Hsing, arrive in Washington as a gift from the People's Republic of China.

Apollo 16, the penultimate lunar mission, is launched.

Mercury Montegos are recalled on 17 April.

Monday 17: Ford in the USA orders a recall of all 1972 Ford Torinos and Mercury Montegos following the discovery of a defect in the rear axles.

Tuesday 18: 43 people are killed when East African Airways flight 720 crashes near Addis Abbaba, Ethiopia.

Wednesday 19: Following a government enquiry, British troops are cleared of blame in the 'Bloody Sunday' shootings in Northern Ireland.

Thursday 20: The US Secretary of State Henry Kissinger meets with Soviet leader Leonid Brezhnev for secret talks in Moscow.

Friday 21: The Apollo 16 Orion lunar module, manned by John Young and Charles Duke, lands on the moon.

Saturday 22: The British TV detective series *New Scotland Yard* is first shown on ITV. It is the first crime drama to be shown on the prime time Saturday slot in place of light entertainment.

Sunday 23: In a national referendum, French voters approve Britain's joining of the Common Market.

Monday 24: The European Economic Community sets up a common currency area, with all member currencies pegged against each other. The system collapses in 1973.

The Polaroid SX-70.

Tuesday 25: The first camera to produce ready-printed photographs instantly, the Polaroid SX-70, goes on sale.

George Sanders dies on 25 April.

The actor George Sanders commits suicide aged 65. His suicide note reads 'I am leaving because I am bored.' His final role was as the voice of the tiger Shere Khan in Disney's *The Jungle Book.*

Wednesday 26: The first Lockheed L-1011 jet liner is launched.

Thursday 27: Alene B Duerk becomes the first woman admiral in the US Navy.

Kwame Nkrumah, first President of Ghana, dies aged 62.

Friday 28: Astronomer Joseph L Brady publishes calculations suggesting the existence of a tenth planet beyond Pluto. The possibility is later ruled out.

Saturday 29: Five months of tribal warfare breaks out between the rival Hutu and Tutsi peoples in Burundi.

Sunday 30: King Ntare V of Burundi is assassinated following the outbreak of tribal warfare.

May 1972

FBI boss J Edgar Hoover dies on 2 May, having run the organisation since 1924.

Monday 1: Hutu rebels in Burundi set up the short-lived People's Republic of Martyazo.

Tuesday 2: The first fibre optic cable is patented.

J Edgar Hoover, director of the FBI since its inception in 1924, dies aged 77.

Wednesday 3: The guitarist Les Harvey, 27, of the group Stone the Crows, is killed on stage by an improperly earthed microphone while performing in front of a crowd of 1200 people in Swansea, Wales.

The Church of England fails to agree a union with the Methodist Church.

Thursday 4: The Paris Peace Talks break down after North Vietnam refuses to negotiate further with the USA and South Vietnam.

Friday 5: Two US airliners are hijacked on the same day: Eastern

The seal of the Japanese Ryukyu Islands and Okinawa. US occupation ends on 15 May.

Airlines flight 175 from Allentown, Pennsylvania and Western Airlines flight 407 from Salt Lake City, Utah. Both hijackers are eventually captured.

Saturday 6: Leeds United wins the FA Cup Final at Wembley Stadium with a 1-0 victory over Arsenal.

Sunday 7: The serial killer Edmund Kemper, 23, kills two young hitch-hikers in California, beginning a year-long murder spree.

Monday 8: President Nixon announces a US naval blockade of North Vietnam's ports, laying mines to prevent access.

Tuesday 9: Israeli special forces storm a hijacked Belgian jet at Tel Aviv airport, freeing all 97 passengers.

Wednesday 10: In a national referendum, voters in the Republic of Ireland choose to join the European Community.

Thursday 11: 83 people are killed when the British steamer STV *Royston Grange* collides with the oil tanker *Tien Chee* in fog off the coast of Uruguay.

Friday 12: Eight people are killed in flash flooding in Texas.

Saturday 13: The first successful use of a laser-guided bomb takes place when USAF planes destroy the Thanh Hoa Bridge in North Vietnam.

Sunday 14: Sir John Warburton Paul becomes the last Governor of the Bahamas before the island's independence in 1973.

Laslzo Toth is restrained after attacking a statue in St Peter's, Rome, on 21 May.

Monday 15: After 26 years of US rule, the island of Okinawa is returned to Japanese administration.

Tuesday 16: The International Money Market opens in Chicago. It is the world's first derivatives exchange, allowing speculation on currency movements.

Wednesday 17: Milan's police commissioner Luigi Calabresi is assassinated, most probably on the orders of the far-left Lotta Continua group.

Thursday 18: The Sea Bed Treaty against the use of nuclear weapons on the ocean floor goes into effect.

HM Queen Elizabeth II meets her uncle, the former King Edward VIII, for the last time.

British special forces are airlifted on to the RMS *Queen Elizabeth II* liner in mid-Atlantic after a bomb threat which turns out to be bogus.

Friday 19: The National Eagle Scout Association is formed in the USA for Eagle Scouts, the equivalent of Queen's Scouts in the British Commonwealth.

Saturday 20: The golfer Jane Blalock is accused of cheating in the USA's Bluegrass Invitational tournament in Prospect, Kentucky. She is cleared of charges three years later.

Sunday 21: In St Peter's in Rome, Michaelangelo's sculpture of Christ and the Virgin Mary, Pieta, is seriously damaged by a mentally deranged man believing himself to be Jesus. The man, Laszlo Toth, is later committed to an asylum.

Monday 22: The British Dominion of Ceylon becomes the Republic of Sri Lanka.

Britain's Poet Laureate, Cecil Day-Lewis (father of actor Daniel Day-Lewis), dies aged 68.

The actress Margaret Rutherford, famous for her portrayal of Miss Marple, dies aged 80.

Tuesday 23: Richard Nixon becomes the first US President to meet in Moscow with his Soviet counterpart, Nikolai Podgorny.

Wednesday 24: West Germany formally relinquishes its claim on all territory lost to the USSR and Poland during the Second World War.

Britain's M6 motorway is completed.

US President Richard Nixon (left) and Soviet leader Leonid Brezhnev sign the SALT 1 arms limitation treaty on 26 March.

Thursday 25: The first computer-controlled flight system on an aeroplane is tested on a Vought F-8 Crusader, using a computer designed for Apollo space missions.

Britain's former king, HRH the Duke of Windsor *(shown with the Duchess of Windsor and US President Nixon)* dies on 28 May.

Friday 26: The historic arms limitation treaty SALT 1 is signed in Moscow by US President Richard Nixon and Soviet premier Leonid Brezhnev.

Saturday 27: Mark Donohue wins the Indianapolis 500 motor race.

Sunday 28: The Duke of Windsor, formerly the King-Emperor Edward VIII who abdicated from the British throne in 1936, dies aged 77.

Monday 29: The US-Soviet summit ends in Moscow with further agreements to restrict arms proliferation and prevent future conflicts.

Tuesday 30: 26 people are killed by Japanese Red Army terrorists in an attack at Lod Airport in Tel Aviv, Israel.

Five children are killed when the Big Dipper roller coaster derails in Battersea Park, London. The accident leads to the permanent closure of the ride, which is the last remaining attraction from the 1951 Festival of Britain.

Wednesday 31: The US Corona spy satellite programme ends after 145 missions.

June
1972

Thursday 1: Andreas Baader, leader of the Baader-Meinhof far-left terrorist gang, is arrested in Munich, Germany.

Alice Cooper releases the album *School's Out.*

Friday 2: Major Richard Locher, USAF, is rescued after being shot down and spending a record 23 days behind enemy lines in Vietnam.

Saturday 3: Sally Priesand becomes the first woman in America to be ordained as a rabbi.

Alice Cooper releases the album *School's Out* **on 1 June.**

Sunday 4: The political activist Angela Davis is acquitted by a jury of involvement in the murder of a judge in California in 1970.

Monday 5: The UN Conference on the Human Environment, the largest ecological conference to this date, takes place in Stockholm, Sweden.

The funeral of the Duke of Windsor takes place in St George's Chapel, Windsor.

Tuesday 6: 426 miners are killed in an explosion in Hwange, Rhodesia.

A US patent is granted to IBM for the first 'floppy disk.'

Wednesday 7: The 1950s musical *Grease* begins the first of 3388 performances on Broadway.

The novelist EM Forster (*A Passage to India*) dies aged 91.

Thursday 8: Photographer Nick Ut captures the image of a young South Vietnamese girl, Phan Thi Kim Phuc, fleeing a napalm attack after South Vietnamese forces mistakenly bombed her village. The photograph becomes an enduring anti-war symbol.

Friday 9: 238 people are killed when the Canyon Lake Dam bursts at Rapid City, South Dakota.

Above: detail from the iconic photograph of 9 year old Vietnamese girl Phan Thi Kim Phuc, victim of a napalm attack on 8 June.

The eight-inch floppy disk (below left), shown here with later smaller versions, is patented on 6 June.

The novelist EM Forster, author of *A Room With A View* and *A Passage to India*, dies on 7 June.

Saturday 10: In Texas, Barbara Jordan becomes the first black woman to serve as an acting US state governor.

Sunday 11: Six people are killed in a train derailment at Well Hall near Eltham, south London.

Monday 12: Following a sharp increase in terrorist attacks, the British Parliament proposes a clampdown on the availability of explosive materials in Northern Ireland.

Tuesday 13: A senior Soviet agent, Nikolay Grigoryevich Petrov, defects to the USA via the American Embassy in Jakarta, Indonesia.

Wednesday 14: The pesticide DDT is banned in the USA.

86 people are killed when Japan Airlines Flight 471 crashes at New Delhi airport, India.

Thursday 15: Dougal Robertson and his family have their yacht sunk by orca whales in the Pacific. They survive 38 days in a dinghy before being rescued. The experience inspires the 1991 film, *Survive the Savage Sea.*

Friday 16: 107 people are killed when a railway tunnel collapses near Soissons, France.

Saturday 17: Five CIA operatives are arrested after breaking into the headquarters of the Democratic National Committee in Washington DC's Watergate complex. The incident marks the beginning of the Watergate scandal which brings down the Nixon government.

Zinedine Zidane is born on 23 June.

Sunday 18: 118 people are killed when BEA flight 548 crashes shortly after takeoff from London Heathrow; it is the worst British air disaster to this date.

Monday 19: The US Supreme Court rules that the bugging of private citizens without a warrant is unconstitutional.

Tuesday 20: The hotelier Howard Johnson dies aged 75.

Wednesday 21: French pilot Jean Boulet sets the world altitude record for a helicopter at 40,814 ft (12,440m).

Thursday 22: The one millionth Ford Thunderbird car is produced.

Friday 23: US President Richard Nixon is recorded secretly telling the FBI to stop investigation of the Watergate burglary. It is this recording which leads to his resignation in 1974.

The French footballer Zinedine Zidane is born in Marseille.

The Ford Thunderbird: the one millionth model is produced on 22 June.

Saturday 24: A 'skyjacker', Martin Joseph McNally, jumps out of a hijacked American Airlines flight carrying over half a million dollars in ransom money; he loses hold of the money bag while jumping and is later arrested.

Sunday 25: Ten soldiers are killed during a rebel uprising in Mexico.

Monday 26: Roberto Duran of Panama defeats Ken Buchanan in New York's Madison Square Garden to become World Lightweight boxing champion.

Tuesday 27: The American computer games manufacturer Atari is founded.

The logo of Atari, founded on 27 June.

Wednesday 28: The Simla Summit of peace talks between India and Pakistan takes place in Simla, India's former summer capital.

Thursday 29: The landmark case of Furman v Georgia ends capital punishment in the USA; the death penalty is restored in some states from 1977.

Friday 30: The first 'leap second' takes place, as one second is added to the world's atomic clocks to make up for anomalies in the earth's orbit.

July 1972

Zero Mostel stars as Tevye in *Fiddler on the Roof*, which ends its Broadway run on 1 July.

Saturday 1: The first official 'Gay Pride' march takes place in London.

Sunday 2: The musical *Fiddler on the Roof* closes on Broadway after 3242 performances.

Monday 3: The Simla Agreement is signed, committing India and Pakistan to the peaceful resolution of disputes and limiting military activity on their borders.

Tuesday 4: North and South Korea announce plans for reunification; the plans are abandoned in 1973.

Wednesday 5: Two hijackers are shot dead after FBI agents storm a plane at San Francisco airport; the *Bonanza* actor Victor Sen Young is wounded in the shooting.

Thursday 6: The actor Brandon de Wilde, best known for his role as Joey in *Shane*, dies aged 30 in a car accident.

Friday 7: King Talal of Jordan dies aged 63.

Secret talks take place in London between members of the IRA and the British government, represented by the Secretary of State for Northern Ireland, William Whitelaw.

Saturday 8: A $750m grain purchase deal by the USSR from the USA is announced.

Sunday 9: The body of Ghanaian leader Kwame Nkrumah is returned to his homeland from Romania, where he died while undergoing surgery.

Monday 10: The largest single act of sabotage in US naval history takes place when Seamen Apprentice Jeffrey Allison sets fire to the USS *Forrestal* in Norfolk, Virginia, causing $7m worth of damage.

Tuesday 11: The World Chess Championship match begins in Reykjavik, with US challenger Bobby Fischer pitted against defending USSR champion Boris Spassky.

Wednesday 12: The Intersputnik Treaty to promote telecommunications between eastern bloc countries goes into effect.

On 17 July the USS *Warrington* becomes the only American ship to be sunk in the Vietnam War.

On 15 July Jane Fonda is photographed on a tour of North Vietnam; she is widely criticised and her career never recovers. In 2005 she apologises for the incident.

King Jigme of Bhutan dies on 21 July.

Thursday 13: The House of Commons narrowly approves Britain's entry into the European Economic Community.

Friday 14: George McGovern is announced as the Democratic Party nominee for the US Presidential elections.

Saturday 15: Pioneer 10 becomes the first man-made object to travel through the asteroid belt.

The actress and peace activist Jane Fonda is photographed making a controversial visit to a North Vietnamese gun emplacement in Hanoi.

Sunday 16: Demetrios I becomes the primate of the Eastern Orthodox Church.

Monday 17: The USS *Warrington* becomes the only US battleship to be sunk in the Vietnam War, after it is hit by US mines which had washed away from their moorings in North Vietnam.

Tuesday 18: Egypt's President Sadat orders all 20,000 Soviet advisors and other personnel to leave the country.

Wednesday 19: Nine members of Britain's Special Air Service (SAS) under the command of Captain

A doctor from the US Centers for Disease Controls (CDC) injects a participant in the now infamous Tuskegee Study, in which syphilis sufferers had treatment withheld. The scandal breaks on 25 July.

Mike Kealy, successful foil a coup attempt by 250 paramilitaries in Oman.

Thursday 20: The first talks between China and Japan since the end of the Second World War begin in Tokyo.

The USA's Lynne Cox, 15, becomes the first person to swim the English Channel in less than ten hours (9 hours 57 minutes).

Friday 21: Nine people are killed in a series of IRA attacks in Belfast which become known as 'Bloody Friday'.

King Jigme of Bhutan dies aged 44.

Saturday 22: The Soviet space probe Venera 8 lands on Venus and transmits data for 50 minutes before temperatures of 470C (900F) cause it to shut down.

Sunday 23: NASA's first Landsat mapping satellite is launched into orbit.

Monday 24: The prototype of the antidepressant drug Prozac is first created.

Tuesday 25: *The Washington Star* breaks the story of the Tuskegee Study, a secret medical experiment in which over 100 men had treatment for syphilis withheld. The survivors receive US$10m in compensation in 1974.

Wednesday 26: Rockwell International is granted the contract for the construction of NASA's Space Shuttle.

Thursday 27: The House of Lords passes the United Reformed Church Bill, combining the Presbyterian Church of England and the Congregational Church of England and Wales.

Friday 28: A national dock strike begins in the UK, leading to the declaration of a State of Emergency in August.

Saturday 29: A Soviet attempt to launch a space station ends in failure as the rocket crashes shortly after take-off.

Sunday 30: The Associated Press sets up the first outside news link with the People's Republic of China.

Monday 31: Operation Motorman begins as 13,000 British troops are sent into the trouble spots of Northern Ireland, greatly reducing the number of terror attacks over the coming months.

August 1972

Tuesday 1: The first article on the Watergate Scandal by the investigative reporters Carl Bernstein and Bob Woodward appears in the *Washington Post*.

Wednesday 2: A political union between the nations of Libya and Egypt is announced. The merger, which never takes place, would have created the ninth largest country in the world.

Bobby Fischer.

Thursday 3: The USSR introduces a 25,000 Rouble exit tax for any Jews wishing to emigrate.

Friday 4: The chess player Bobby Fischer achieves an ELO (chess score) of 2789.7 in the World Chess Championship in Reykjavik, Iceland. The record lasts for 22 years.

Saturday 5: The London Rock and Roll Show takes place, the first major musical event to be held at London's Wembley Stadium.

Paul Nicholas stars in the title role in *Jesus Christ Superstar* from 9 August.

Sunday 6: The Ugandan dictator Idi Amin announces that all 50,000 persons of Asian descent in the country are to be expelled.

Monday 7: The most powerful solar flare recorded on Earth is observed at 15.19 GMT.

Tuesday 8: The US Navy announces that women will be allowed serve on board its ships alongside men.

Wednesday 9: The musical *Jesus Christ Superstar,* by Tim Rice and Andrew Lloyd-Webber makes its West End debut.

Thursday 10: A meteor comes within 36 miles of the Earth and is visible for over a minute over Utah.

Friday 11: Andrew Topping, 27, is arrested in New York City after planning to assassinate US President Richard Nixon.

Saturday 12: The first American Hairless Terrier is born.

Sunday 13: The 21st US Infantry, the last American ground patrol regiment in Vietnam, is stood down. Air and sea-based units remain in the country until 1973.

An American Hairless Terrier: the first of the breed is born on 12 August.

Monday 14: In the worst German air disaster to this date, 156 people are killed when an Interflug airliner crashes near Berlin.

Tuesday 15: The actor Ben Affleck is born in Berkeley, California.

Wednesday 16: An attempted coup in Morocco, including an assassination attempt on King Hassan II, ends in failure.

Thursday 17: Indonesia announces changes to its alphabet, resulting in the capital Djakarta changing to Jakarta.

**Ben Affleck
is born on 15 August.**

Friday 18: A telephone link between North and South Korea is re-established, for the first time since communications were broken off in 1950.

Saturday 19: US Secretary of State Henry Kissinger and South Vietnamese President Nguyen Van Thieu begin talks on the ending of the Vietnam War.

Sunday 20: A fundamentalist American Mormon preacher, Joel LeBaron, is shot dead on the orders of his brother, Ervil, the leader of a rival sect. He is eventually captured in 1981.

Monday 21: The Copernicus satellite, an orbiting astronomical telescope, is launched. It remains in service until 1979.

Tuesday 22: A bungled bank robbery, the inspiration for the film *Dog Day Afternoon*, takes place in Brooklyn, New York City.

The Copernicus satellite is launched on 21 August.

Neil Diamond.

Wednesday 23: Kakuei Tanaka, Prime Minister of Japan, accepts a bribe to award government contracts to Lockheed aircraft. He is exposed and prosecuted in 1976.

Thursday 24: Neil Diamond records his platinum selling album *Hot August Night.*

Friday 25: The Wal-Mart chain of stores is floated on the New York Stock Exchange.

Saturday 26: The 1972 Summer Olympics begins in Munich.

The solo yachtsman Sir Francis Chichester dies aged 70.

Sunday 27: 400 celebrities including Frank Sinatra and John Wayne attend a gala event at the Western White House hosted by President and Mrs Nixon.

Monday 28: HRH Prince William of Gloucester, cousin of HM the Queen, is killed in an air crash aged 30.

Above: Cameron Diaz is born on 30 August.
Right: HRH Prince William is killed on 27 August.

Tuesday 29: US President Nixon announces that the number of troops remaining in Vietnam will be reduced to 27,000 by 1 December, a 95% reduction since the peak of the war in 1969.

Wednesday 30: A group of militant Hispanic-Americans seize control of Santa Catalina Island off the Californian coast. They are eventually evicted on 22 September.

The actress Cameron Diaz is born in San Diego, California.

Thursday 31: Bobby Fischer becomes World Chess Champion when he defeats Boris Spassky in the 'chess match of the century' in Reykjavik, Iceland.

US swimmers Lyn Skrifvars (left) and Mary Montgomery take a break during the Olympics in Munich.

September 1972

Woody Woodpecker taps out on 1 September.

Friday 1: The last Woody Woodpecker cartoon, *Bye Bye Blackboard*, is released.

The school leaving age in the UK is raised from 15 to 16.

Saturday 2: Egypt, Libya and Syria form the Federation of Arab Republics.

Sunday 3: Lon Nol's Social Republican Party is victorious in Cambodia's Khmer Republic elections.

Monday 4: The swimmer Mark Spitz (USA) becomes the first athlete to win seven medals in a single Olympic Games.

The New Price is Right, hosted by Bob Barker, is launched on US television.

Tuesday 5: Palestinian terrorists kill two Israeli olympic team members in Munich, and take nine others hostage.

Wednesday 6: German police make a bungled attempt to end

Bob Barker hosts
The New Price is Right
on 4 September.

the hostage crisis at the Olympics, resulting in terrorists killing nine hostages.

Thursday 7: Prime Minister Indira Gandhi authorises Indian's nuclear weapons programme; the first atom bomb is tested in 1974.

Friday 8: The Israeli Air Force bombs terrorist strongholds in Syria and Lebanon in reprisal for the Munich attacks on 6 September.

Saturday 9: The world's longest cave-passageway, measuring 144.4 miles, is discovered in Flint Ridge, Kentucky.

Sunday 10: Brazil's Emerson Fittipaldi becomes, at 25, the world's youngest Formula One champion when he wins the Italian Grand Prix.

Monday 11: San Francisco's Bay Area Rapid Transit (BART) railway goes into operation.

Tuesday 12: The Second Cod War starts when the Icelandic Coastguard vessel *Aegir* attacks two British trawlers.

Wednesday 13: 54 North Korean Red Cross workers meet their counterparts in South Korea in the first cross-border visit by officials since 1953.

The Waltons is first broadcast on 14 September.

Thursday 14: West Germany and Poland restore diplomatic relations, severed since 1939.

The long-running CBS TV series *The Waltons* is first broadcast.

Friday 15: in the Watergate scandal, a federal grand jury indicts the five men alleged to have burgled the Democratic Party offices in June.

The comedian Jimmy Carr is born in Hounslow, Middlesex.

Jimmy Carr is born on 15 September.

The former Archbishop of Canterbury Geoffrey Fisher dies aged 85.

Saturday 16: 103 people are killed when the Colgante Bridge collapses in Naga City, Philippines.

The comedy series *The Bob Newhart Show* is first broadcast on CBS TV.

Sunday 17: *M*A*S*H*, the long-running comedy series set in the Korean War, is first broadcast on US TV.

Left: the comedy series *M*A*S*H*, set in the Korean War but in effect a satire of the Vietnam War, is first broadcast on 17 September.

Monday 18: Japan's foreign minister Zentaro Kosaka makes a formal apology for Japanese atrocities in China in the 1930s and 40s.

The first Ugandan Asians arrive in the UK, after their expulsion by Idi Amin.

Tuesday 19: Diplomat Ami Schachori is killed by a letter bomb sent to the Israeli Embassy in London.

Liam Gallagher is born on 21 October.

Wednesday 20: Muhammed Ali retains his World Heavyweight boxing title in a bout with former champion Floyd Patterson.

Thursday 21: Martial law is declared in the Philippines.

The singer Liam Gallagher of Oasis is born in Manchester, England.

Friday 22: The disinfectant hexachlorophene, commonly found in cosmetics and baby products, is banned in the USA after studies show it can cause brain damage in infants.

On 26 September the presidency of South Vietnam's Nguyen Van Thieu (shown with US President Richard Nixon in 1969) is saved.

Saturday 23: 31 tourists are killed in a restaurant fire on the Greek island of Rhodes.

Sunday 24: 23 people are killed when a USAF jet fighter crashes into an ice-cream parlour in Sacramento, California.

Monday 25: Norway votes against joining the Common Market in a national referendum.

Gwyneth Paltrow is born on 27 October.

David Cassidy hits number one on 30 October.

Tuesday 26: A major breakthrough in peace talks takes place when North Vietnam drops its demands for South Vietnam's President Nguyen Van Thieu to resign as a condition of ceasefire.

Wednesday 27: The actress Gwyneth Paltrow is born in Los Angeles, California.

Thursday 28: The US Army pardons 167 soldiers (166 of them posthumously) who were dishonourably discharged after being falsely accused of involvement in the death of two civilians in Brownsville, Texas, in 1906.

Friday 29: Vasil Mzhavanadze, leader of Soviet Georgia, is removed from office on the orders of Moscow and replaced by Eduard Shevardnadze.

Saturday 30: *How Can I Be Sure?* by David Cassidy reaches number one in the UK singles charts.

October 1972

Peter Sellers appears in *The Last Goon Show of All* on 5 October.

Sunday 1: Florida becomes the first US state to reinstitute the death penalty.

Monday 2: In a national referendum, Danes vote 63% in favour of joining the EEC.

Tuesday 3: The Anti-Ballistic Missile Treaty on arms reduction between the USA and USSR goes into effect.

Wednesday 4: The title 'Ms' is used for the first time by a US Congresswoman.

Thursday 5: BBC radio broadcasts *The Last Goon Show of All*, re-uniting the comedians Peter Sellers, Spike Milligan, Harry Secombe and Michael Bentine for the first time since 1960.

Friday 6: Six schoolgirls and their teacher are kidnapped in Faraday, in the Australian state of Victoria. A ransom of one million Australian dollars is demanded, but the girls manage to escape. Two local men are eventually convicted.

October 1972

Saturday 7: US President Nixon proposes a $250 billion cap on public spending rather than impose tax increases.

Sunday 8: A provisional peace treaty is brokered in Vietnam by US Secretary of State Henry Kissinger. Negotiations, however, break down on 30 October.

Sir John Betjeman becomes Poet Laureate on 10 October.

Monday 9: One of the great theatrical flops of the decade, *Dude: The Highway Life* by Jerome Ragni opens on Broadway. It closes after just 16 performances with losses of $800,000.

Tuesday 10: Sir John Betjeman is appointed Poet Laureate.

Wednesday 11: The case of Roe *v* Wade, which eventually results in the legalisation of abortion, is re-opened in the US Supreme Court.

David Carradine stars in *Kung Fu*, first broadcast on 14 October.

Thursday 12: Troops from Portuguese Guinea invade the west African country of Senegal in a hunt for terrorists; the action is condemned by the UN.

Friday 13: 174 people are killed in the worst aviation disaster to this date, when an Aeroflot jet crashes near the Russian city of Krasnaya Polyana.

Saturday 14: The action-adventure series *Kung Fu* starring David Carradine is first shown on US TV.

Sunday 15: A cow is killed by a meteorite in Venezuela, the only recorded instance of an animal being killed by space debris.

Monday 16: The first direct electronic transfer of funds between banks takes place in California.

The long running soap opera *Emmerdale Farm* is first broadcast in Britain.

Two US politicians, Hale Boggs and Nick Begich, go missing along with their pilot and aide when their plane crashes in Alaska; no trace of them is ever found.

Eminem is born on 17 October.

Tuesday 17: Martial law is declared in South Korea.

The rapper Eminem (Marshall Mathers) is born in St Joseph, Missouri.

Wednesday 18: The USCSR agrees to repay $722m in loans made by the USA during and after the Second World War.

Thursday 19: A gun battle takes place between police on the Philippines island of Lubang and two of the last 'hold outs' (Japanese soldiers in hiding since the end of the Second World War). One soldier is killed and the other surrenders in 1974.

The village of Arncliffe in Yorkshire is used as the location of *Emmerdale Farm*, first broadcast on 16 October.

October 1972

The first portrayal of a living member of the Royal Family (HM Queen Elizabeth the Queen Mother) takes place, when the play *Crown Matrimonial* opens at London's Haymarket Theatre.

The Access card is launched on 23 October.

Friday 20: Britain's Rodney Porter and the USA's Gerald M Edelmen are awarded the Nobel Prize for Medicine for their work on antibody research.

Saturday 21: Somalia becomes the first country since 1940 to Romanise its alphabet.

Sunday 22: Four Turkish terrorists force a jet liner to divert from Ankara to Bulgaria where they claim political asylum.

Monday 23: Access credit cards are introduced in the UK.

Tuesday 24: Jackie Robinson, the first black player in major league US baseball, dies aged 53.

Wednesday 25: The *Washington Post* accuses White House Chief of Staff Harry Robbins Haldeman of secretly financing political sabotage in the 1972 Presidential election campaign.

Thursday 26: Igor Sikorsky, designer of the first modern helicopter, dies aged 83.

Friday 27: Elton John's song *Crocodile Rock* is released. It goes on to become his first hit record.

Left: Elton John.

The Airbus A300, which makes its first flight on 28 October.

The Mars probe Mariner 9 is switched off after transmitting over 7000 images of the Red Planet.

Saturday 28: The Airbus A300 flies for the first time.

Sunday 29: Lufthansa flight 615 is hijacked by Palestinian terrorists who demand the release of the three remaining Munich olympics attackers. The West German authorities agree to the demands.

Monday 30: A stalemate with no overall victor occurs in the closest-run federal election in Canada's history.

Tuesday 31: 22 US servicemen are killed when their Chinook helicopter is downed in the last major air attack of the Vietnam War.

November 1972

Wednesday 1: The poet Ezra Pound dies aged 87.

Thursday 2: Canada's New Democrat party forms a coalition with the Liberals to ensure Pierre Trudeau becomes Prime Minister following the close-fought election of 30 October.

Friday 3: The first mutiny in US Navy history takes place on board the USS *Constellation*, as 132 sailors refuse to obey orders following an unfair dismissal case.

Saturday 4: The US spy ship *Glomar Explorer* is launched to recover the remains of a Soviet submarine in the Pacific, with the cover story of researching geology.

Sunday 5: Organic farming is given a global boost as The International Federation of Organic Agriculture Movements is founded.

Monday 6: 29 people are killed in a fire on an express train near Fukui, Japan.

Pierre Trudeau forms a coalition government on 2 November.

President Richard Nixon on the campaign trail in Florida before his election victory of 7 November.

Tuesday 7: Richard Nixon is re-elected in a landslide victory in the US Presidential election.

Wednesday 8: HBO the USA's first pay-per-view cable channel, is launched in the USA.

Thursday 9: Canada's first communications satellite, Anek-1, is launched.

Friday 10: Southern Airways flight 49 from Birmingham, Alabama, is hijacked by three men who demand a $10m ransom before ordering the plane to fly to several different destinations.

Saturday 11: Authorities pay only $2m of the ransom demanded by the hijackers of Southern Airways flight 49, and the flight is forced to travel to Cuba.

Sunday 12: The hijackers of Southern Airways flight 49 are arrested on arrival in Cuba. The incident leads to the compulsory screening of all US airline passengers for weapons.

Monday 13: In London, 79 nations sign the Convention on the Prevention of Marine Pollution.

Tuesday 14: The Dow Jones Industrial Average closes at over 1000 points for the first time in its history.

November 1972

Wednesday 15: Pope Paul VI declares that the devil is a 'living being' rather than a metaphor for evil.

Thursday 16: The UNESCO World Heritage Convention is signed, beginning the designation of World Heritage Sites around the world.

Pepsi Cola signs a deal with the USSR, making it the first US consumer product to be produced under licence by the Soviets.

Friday 17: The former Argentinian leader Juan Peron returns to his homeland after 17 years in exile.

Saturday 18: The USS *Sanctuary* becomes the first US Navy ship to allow mixed crews.

The first official national women's association football match takes place between England and Scotland.

Sunday 19: Chancellor Willy Brandt is re-elected in West Germany's federal elections.

Monday 20: A round of high profile US government resignations takes place, including the CIA director Richard Helms.

Tuesday 21: The stunt motorcyclist Stephen Ladd is killed in Epping, near London, while attempting to ride through a 50 yard long tunnel made from burning hay bales for a second time.

Top: Juan Peron returns to Argentina on 17 November. Right: Willy Brandt is re-elected as West Germany's leader on 19 November.

The arcade version of Pong is launched on 29 November.

Wednesday 22: The mass murderer Richard Speck is sentenced to 1200 years in prison, the longest jail term in US history to this date.

Thursday 23: The USSR's fourth and final attempt at testing a rocket capable of a manned lunar mission fails when its N1 rocket explodes at an altitude of 25 miles.

Friday 24: The search for the missing US Congressman Hale Boggs, whose plane went missing over Alaska on 16 October, is called off.

Saturday 25: Norman Kirk's Labour Party is victorious in the New Zealand general election.

Sunday 26: The Norwegian military calls off a two week hunt for a mystery submarine, thought to be a Soviet spying vessel, detected in its waters.

Monday 27: The *Sesame Street* character 'The Count' makes his first TV appearance.

The Count first appears on 27 November.

Tuesday 28: 62 people are killed when Japan Airlines flight 446 crashes shortly after takeoff from Moscow.

Wednesday 29: Atari releases the arcade version of the computer game Pong, the first arcade game to achieve commercial success.

Thursday 30: The author Sir Compton McKenzie (*Whisky Galore*) dies aged 89.

December 1972

Gough Whitlam wins on 2 December.

Friday 1: India and Pakistan repatriate all prisoners taken during the Indo-Pakistan War of 1971.

Saturday 2: The Labor Party led by Gough Whitlam wins the Australian federal elections.

Sunday 3: 155 people are killed when a Spantax Airlines flight crashes shortly after takeoff from Tenerife.

Monday 4: A military coup takes place in Honduras.

Tuesday 5: Compulsory screening of all passengers and hand luggage at airports in the USA is mandated for 5 January 1973.

Wednesday 6: Work begins on the restoration of the Borobudur temple in Java, a UNESCO world heritage site.

Thursday 7: The last US conscripts are called up.

Eugene Cernan is the last man to walk on the moon, on 11 December.

The last NASA lunar mission, Apollo 17, is launched.

Friday 8: Florida becomes the first US state to reintroduce capital punishment.

Saturday 9: Pilot Marten Hartwell is rescued after spending 31 days stranded in the arctic following a plane crash.

Sunday 10: Britain's John Hicks is awarded the Nobel Prize for Economics.

Monday 11: Eugene Cernan becomes the last man to walk on the moon as Apollo 17 lands on the lunar surface.

Tuesday 12: The first Haitian boat refugees arrive in the USA.

Wednesday 13: Vietnam War peace talks break down as North Vietnam's negotiators walk out.

Thursday 14: The last Apollo mission leaves the moon.

Friday 15: UNEP, the United Nations Environment Program is launched.

Saturday 16: A massacre of 300 civilians takes place in Wiriyamu, Mozambique, allegedly carried out by Portuguese troops during a counter-insurgency campaign.

December 1972

Vanessa Paradis is born on 22 December.

Sunday 17: The Line of Control, or demilitarized zone, goes into operation on the Indo-Pakistan border.

Monday 18: A major US bombing offensive, Operation Linebacker II, goes into operation in Vietnam following the breakdown of peace talks.

Tuesday 19: 144 million litres of oil are spilled when the tanker Sea Star collides with another vessel in the Persian Gulf.

Wednesday 20: The Northrop M2-F3, an experimental wingless or 'lifting body' aircraft makes its final test flight before the project is abandoned.

Thursday 21: East and West Germany sign a treaty to 'promote good-neighbourly relations.'

Friday 22: The singer and actress Vanessa Paradis is born in Paris, France.

Saturday 23: Over 10,000 people are killed when a devastating earthquake hits Managua, Nicaragua.

Sunday 24: A 36-hour Christmas ceasefire begins in Vietnam.

The bodybuilder Charles Atlas dies aged 80.

Left: Charles Atlas, who dies on 24 December, achieved fame with his body-building courses.

Monday 25: The USSR makes it illegal for dissidents to meet with foreigners in order to 'disseminate false information.'

Tuesday 26: Harry S Truman, 33rd President of the United States (1945-1953) dies aged 88.

Wednesday 27: All US petrol stations are required to introduced unleaded petrol by July 1974.

Thursday 28: Kim Il-Sung becomes President of North Korea.

Friday 29: 101 people are killed when Eastern Airlines flight 401 crashes in the Florida Everglades.

Saturday 30: North Vietnam agrees to continue ceasefire negotiations after a heavy US bombing campaign.

Top: Kim Il-Sung becomes President of North Korea on 28 December.
Above: Harry S Truman dies on 26 December.

Sunday 31: An extra second or leap second is added to atomic clocks at the end of the year to balance with solar time, making 1972 the longest year in history.

Other titles from Montpelier Publishing:

A Little Book of Limericks:
Funny Rhymes for all the Family
ISBN 9781511524124

Scottish Jokes: A Wee Book of
Clean Caledonian Chuckles
ISBN 9781495297366

The Old Fashioned Joke Book:
Gags and Funny Stories
ISBN 9781514261989

Non-Religious Funeral Readings:
Philosophy and Poetry for Secular
Services
ISBN 9781500512835

Large Print Jokes: Hundreds of
Gags in Easy-to-Read Type
ISBN 9781517775780

**Spiritual Readings for Funerals
and Memorial Services**
ISBN 9781503379329

Victorian Murder: True Crimes,
Confessions and Executions
ISBN 9781530296194

Large Print Prayers: A Prayer for
Each Day of the Month
ISBN 9781523251476

**A Little Book of Ripping Riddles
and Confounding Conundrums**
ISBN 9781505548136

Vinegar uses: over 150 ways to use
vinegar
ISBN 0701512136623

Large Print Wordsearch:
100 Puzzles in Easy-to-Read Type
ISBN 9781517638894

The Pipe Smoker's Companion
ISBN 9781500441401

The Book of Church Jokes
ISBN 9781507620632

Bar Mitzvah Notebook
ISBN 9781976007781

Jewish Jokes
ISBN 9781514845769

Large Print Address Book
ISBN 9781539820031

How to Cook Without a Kitchen:
Easy, Healthy and Low-Cost Meals
9781515340188

Large Print Birthday Book
ISBN 9781544670720

Retirement Jokes
ISBN 9781519206350

Take my Wife: Hilarious Jokes of
Love and Marriage
ISBN 9781511790956

Welsh Jokes: A Little Book of
Wonderful Welsh Wit
ISBN 9781511612241

1001 Ways to Save Money: Thrifty
Tips for the Fabulously Frugal!
ISBN 9781505432534

Available online at Amazon

Printed in Great Britain
by Amazon